Carnivore Air fryer cookbook

Elevate Your Cooking Game with the Air Fryer

Daphne Anderson

Copyright
© **2024 by Daphne Anderson**

All rights reserved. Without the previous written permission of the publisher, no part of this book may be copied, distributed, or transmitted in any form or by any means, including photocopying, recording, or other electronic or mechanical techniques. The only exceptions to this rule are short excerpts that are integrated into critical reviews and some other nonprofit uses that are authorized under copyright law.

TABLE OF CONTENTS

- INTRODUCTION TO AIR FRYING — 6
- BENEFITS OF CARNIVORE AIR FRYING — 7
- AIR FRYER BEEF RECIPES — 8
  - Air Fryer Steak Bites — 8
  - Air Fryer Bacon — 9
  - Air Fryer Ground Beef — 10
  - Air Fryer Beef Jerky — 11
  - Air Fryer Beef Fajitas — 12
  - Air Fryer Beef Brisket — 13
  - Air Fryer Beef Short Ribs — 14
  - Air Fryer Beef Short Ribs — 15
  - Air Fryer Beef Liver — 16
  - Air Fryer Beef Tongue — 17
- PORK RECIPES — 18
  - Air Fryer Pork Chops — 18
  - Crispy Air Fried Pork Belly — 19
  - Garlic Parmesan Pork Bites — 20
  - Cajun Spiced Pork Tenderloin — 21
  - Honey Mustard Glazed Pork Ribs — 22
  - Italian Herb Air Fryer Pork Loin — 23
  - Teriyaki Pork Skewers — 24
  - Chili Lime Pork Carnitas — 25
  - Bacon-Wrapped Air Fryer Pork Tenderloin — 26
  - Spicy Sriracha Pork Wings — 27
- CHICKEN RECIPES — 28
  - Carnivore Fried Chicken — 28
  - Air Fryer Keto Chicken Wings — 29
  - Air Fryer Garlic Parmesan Chicken Thighs: — 30
  - Air Fryer Spicy Chicken Legs: — 31
  - Air Fryer Chicken Fajitas — 32
  - Air Fryer Chicken Skewers — 33
  - Air Fryer Whole Chicken: — 34

- Air Fryer Chicken Nuggets: --- 35
- Air Fryer Chicken Tenders --- 36
- Air Fryer Buffalo Chicken Wings --- 37
- Air Fryer BBQ Chicken: --- 38

LAMB RECIPES --- 39
- Pan-Seared Lamb Chops with Garlic Butter --- 39
- Keto Lamb Kofta --- 40
- Air Fryer Lamb Merguez Sausage: --- 41
- Air Fryer Lamb Kebabs --- 42
- Air Fryer Ground Lamb Burgers --- 43
- Air Fryer Lamb Sliders: --- 44
- Air Fryer Lamb Gyro Meat: --- 45
- Air Fryer Lamb Chops with Bacon --- 46
- Air Fryer Lamb Kofta Kebabs --- 47

SEAFOOD RECIPES --- 48
- Air Fryer Garlic Herb Salmon --- 48
- Air Fryer Parmesan Crusted Tilapia --- 49
- Air Fryer Cajun Shrimp --- 50
- Air Fryer Lobster Tails with Garlic Butter --- 51
- Air Fryer Scallops with Lemon and Herbs --- 52
- Air Fryer Calamari with Marinara Sauce --- 53
- Air Fryer Fish Sticks --- 54
- Air Fryer Crab Cakes --- 55
- Air Fryer Oysters Rockefeller --- 56
- Air Fryer Spicy Tuna Steaks --- 57

GAME RECIPES --- 58
- Seared Bison Steak with Herb Butter --- 58
- Burger Bowls --- 59
- Meatballs with Creamy Sauce --- 60
- Meat Skewers with Chimichurri --- 61
- Breakfast Scramble --- 62
- Meat Jerky --- 63

SIDE DISHES --- 64

- Crispy Bacon — 64
- Air Fryer Sausage Links — 65
- Beef Jerky — 66
- Pork Rinds — 67
- Deviled Eggs — 68
- Garlic Parmesan Chicken Wings: — 69
- Salmon with Herb Butter — 70

SAUCES AND DIPS — 71
- Bang Bang Sauce — 71
- Buffalo Chicken Dip — 72
- Steak Fajita Marinade — 73
- Teriyaki Sauce — 74
- Garlic Parmesan Sauce — 75
- Honey Garlic Sauce — 76

TIPS AND TRICKS FOR PERFECT AIR FRIED CARNIVORE MEALS — 77
- Conclusion — 78

INTRODUCTION TO AIR FRYING

Welcome to the delicious world of carnivore air frying, where juicy meats meet the magic of air-cooking technology! Prepare to take on a culinary trip that will excite your taste buds and elevate your eating experience to new heights.

As you step into this world, you'll discover the art of air frying, a new cooking method that uses hot air movement to achieve crispy exteriors and soft innards without the need for excessive oil. Embrace the freedom to indulge in your favorite meat treats guilt-free, as the air fryer works its magic to create healthy yet equally delicious versions of your beloved meals.

Picture perfectly seasoned steaks sizzling to perfection, crispy chicken wings with just the right amount of crunch, and juicy burgers dripping with flavor—all achieved with minimal work and maximum flavor. The carnivore air fryer becomes your trusted partner in the kitchen, providing consistent results every time, whether you're a seasoned chef or a cooking beginner.

But it's not just about ease and health benefits; it's also about the sheer joy of experimentation and creation. With the Omnivore air fryer in your hands, the options are endless. From classic cuts of meat to new takes on traditional recipes, you'll find yourself inspired to push the limits of taste and texture.

So, welcome to the omnivore air cooking society, where every meal is a celebration of taste and innovation. Get ready to start on a mouthwatering adventure that will leave you craving more with each delicious bite.

What is carnivore air frying?

Carnivore air frying usually refers to using an air fryer to cook meat-based meals. It's a way of cooking where hot air flows around the food, making a crispy surface while keeping wetness inside, similar to deep-frying but with significantly less oil.

Carnivore air frying can cook various types of meat, including chicken wings, pork chops, steak bites, and even bacon. It's a handy and healthy choice to standard fried ways, as it needs less oil while still getting delicious results. Plus, air fryers are easy to use and clean, making them a popular choice for home cooks looking to enjoy their favorite meat meals with less trouble.

BENEFITS OF CARNIVORE AIR FRYING

1. Healthier Cooking: Air frying needs little to no oil, resulting in lower fat levels compared to standard cooking ways. This can help to better heart health and weight control.

2. Retains Nutrients: Air frying saves more nutrients in meat compared to other cooking methods like boiling or grilling, as it cooks quickly at a high temperature, reducing nutrient loss.

3. Enhanced Flavor: Air frying locks in the natural juices of meat while providing a crispy surface, resulting in a delicious and flavorful dish.

4. Time Efficiency: Air frying is faster than normal oven cooking, making it ideal for busy plans. It preheats quickly and cooks meat in a fraction of the time it takes to bake or roast.

5. Easy Cleanup: Air fryers are usually non-stick and require minimal cleanup. This saves time and effort compared to dealing with dirty pans and splatters from standard cooking ways.

6. Versatility: Air fryers can cook a variety of carnivore-friendly foods, from steak and bacon to chicken wings and pork chops, offering a range of meal choices.

7. Reduced Odors: Air frying produces fewer cooking odors compared to traditional frying ways, making it more pleasant to cook indoors without lasting smells.

8. Consistent Results: Air fryers provide even cooking and consistent results, ensuring that your carnivore meals are always perfectly cooked.

9. Energy Efficiency: Air fryers use less energy compared to standard ovens, helping to lower power bills and environmental effects.

10. Portability: Air fryers are tiny and movable, making them perfect for small homes or for taking along to outdoor parties or camping trips.

AIR FRYER BEEF RECIPES

Air Fryer Steak Bites

Prep Time: 5 minutes Cook Time: 10-15 minutes Total Time: 15-20 minutes Servings: 1

Ingredients:
4 oz grass-fed steak (flank, skirt, or sirloin), cut into bite-sized pieces
1/2 tsp sea salt
1/4 tsp black pepper

Preheat your air fryer to 400°F (200°C) for 5 minutes.

In a bowl, toss the steak bites with salt and pepper.

Arrange the steak bites in a single layer in the air fryer basket, ensuring they are not touching.

Air fry for 10-15 minutes, or until desired doneness is reached. For medium-rare, aim for an internal temperature of 130-135°F (54-57°C).

Once cooked, remove the steak bites from the air fryer and let them rest for a few minutes before serving.

Nutritional Information (per serving):
Calories: 230
Fat: 17g
Protein: 25g
Carbs: 0g
Net Carbs: 0g

Air Fryer Bacon

Prep Time: 2 minutes Cook Time: 5-12 minutes (depending on thickness and desired crispiness) Total Time: 7-14 minutes Servings: 1-2

Ingredients:
4-6 slices of bacon (choose uncured, sugar-free bacon for the carnivore diet)

Preheat your air fryer to 350°F (175°C).
Arrange the bacon slices in a single layer in the air fryer basket, making sure they don't overlap significantly.
Cook for 5-7 minutes for thin-cut bacon and 8-12 minutes for thick-cut bacon, or until desired crispiness is reached.
Flip the bacon halfway through cooking for even browning (optional).
Once cooked, remove the bacon from the air fryer and transfer it to a paper towel-lined plate to drain any excess grease.

Nutritional Information (per serving, based on 2 slices of thick-cut bacon):
Calories: 180
Fat: 13g
Protein: 8g
Carbohydrates: 0g
Sodium: 120mg

Air Fryer Ground Beef

Prep Time: 5 minutes Cook Time: 8-10 minutes Total Time: 13-15 minutes Servings: 2

Ingredients:

1 pound ground beef (80/20 or higher fat content)

Sea salt

Black pepper

Preheat your air fryer to 400°F (200°C) for 5 minutes.

While the air fryer is preheating, break up the ground beef into small crumbles.

Season generously with sea salt and black pepper to your taste.

Spread the ground beef in a single layer in the air fryer basket, making sure not to overcrowd it.

Cook for 8-10 minutes, or until the ground beef is browned and cooked through. You may need to shake the basket halfway through cooking to ensure even browning.

Drain any excess grease from the bottom of the basket using paper towels.

Serve immediately.

Nutritional Information (per serving):

Calories: 450-500

Fat: 40-45g

Protein: 30-35g

Carbs: 0g

Air Fryer Beef Jerky

Prep Time: 15 minutes Cooking Time: 2-3 hours Total Time: 2-3 hours 15 minutes Servings: 4-6

Ingredients:
1 pound lean beef (flank steak, eye of round)
1 tablespoon soy sauce (or coconut aminos for a soy-free option)
1 tablespoon Worcestershire sauce (sugar-free)
1/2 teaspoon black pepper
1/4 teaspoon garlic powder
1/4 teaspoon onion powder

Slice the beef: Freeze the beef for 30 minutes to 1 hour to firm it up for easier slicing. Slice the beef against the grain into thin strips, about 1/4 inch thick.
Marinate: In a bowl, combine the soy sauce, Worcestershire sauce, black pepper, garlic powder, and onion powder. Add the beef strips and toss to coat evenly. Marinate for at least 30 minutes, or up to overnight, in the refrigerator.
Preheat the air fryer: Preheat your air fryer to 210°F (100°C).
Arrange the beef: Pat the beef strips dry with paper towels. Arrange the strips in a single layer on the air fryer basket, ensuring they don't overlap.
Dehydrate: Air fry the beef jerky for 2-3 hours, checking on it every 30 minutes. The jerky is done when it is dry, leathery, and bends without breaking. It should reach an internal temperature of 160°F (71°C).
Cool and store: Let the jerky cool completely before storing it in an airtight container in the refrigerator. It will last for up to 2 weeks.

Nutritional Information (per serving):
Calories: 220
Fat: 15g
Protein: 25g
Carbs: 0g

Air Fryer Beef Fajitas

Prep Time: 5 minutes Cooking Time: 15 minutes Total Time: 20 minutes Servings: 2

Ingredients:
1 pound flank steak, thinly sliced against the grain
1 tablespoon olive oil
1 teaspoon ground cumin
1/2 teaspoon chili powder
Salt and pepper to taste

In a bowl, combine olive oil, cumin, chili powder, salt, and pepper. Toss the steak slices with the spice mixture to coat evenly.
Preheat your air fryer to 400°F (200°C).
Arrange the steak slices in a single layer in the air fryer basket. Avoid overcrowding the basket, cook in batches if needed.
Air fry for 7-8 minutes, or until desired doneness is reached. For medium-rare steak, aim for an internal temperature of 145°F (63°C).
While the steak is cooking, you can optionally warm your tortillas in a separate pan or oven.
Once cooked, remove the steak from the air fryer and let it rest for a few minutes before slicing.
Serve the steak fajitas with your desired toppings, such as guacamole, salsa, and sour cream (not recommended for a strict carnivore diet).

Nutritional Information:
(per serving)
Calories: 450
Fat: 35g
Protein: 50g
Carbs: 0g

Air Fryer Beef Brisket

Prep Time: 5 minutes Cooking Time: 2-3 hours (depending on thickness) Total Time: 2-3 hours and 5 minutes Servings: 4-6

Ingredients:
1.5 - 2 lbs beef brisket flat cut (with fat cap)
Sea salt

Prep: Trim any excess fat from the brisket, leaving a thin layer of fat cap. Pat the brisket dry with paper towels. Generously season the entire brisket with sea salt, making sure to get into the crevices.
Cooking: Preheat your air fryer to 300°F (150°C). Place the brisket, fat cap side down, in the air fryer basket. Cook for 1 hour.
Flip and Raise Temperature: After 1 hour, flip the brisket over and increase the temperature to 325°F (163°C). Cook for another 1-2 hours, or until the internal temperature of the thickest part reaches 195°F (90°C) on a meat thermometer.
Rest: Remove the brisket from the air fryer and let it rest for 10-15 minutes before slicing against the grain.

Nutritional Information: (per serving)
Calories: 450-550 (depending on fat content)
Protein: 70-80g
Fat: 30-40g
Carbs: 0g

Air Fryer Beef Short Ribs

Prep Time: 5 minutes Cook Time: 30-40 minutes Total Time: 35-45 minutes Servings: 2

Ingredients:
1 pound beef short ribs, trimmed of excess fat
Sea salt, to taste

Preheat your air fryer to 400°F (200°C) for 5 minutes.

Pat the beef short ribs dry with paper towels. Season generously with sea salt on all sides.

Place the short ribs in a single layer in the air fryer basket, ensuring they are not touching.

Air fry for 15-20 minutes, then flip the ribs and cook for another 15-20 minutes, or until they reach an internal temperature of 160°F (71°C) for medium-rare or 165°F (74°C) for medium.

Remove from the air fryer and let rest for 5 minutes before serving.

Nutritional Information (per serving):
Calories: 520
Fat: 45g
Protein: 40g
Carbs: 0g

Air Fryer Beef Short Ribs

Prep Time: 5 minutes Cook Time: 30-40 minutes Total Time: 35-45 minutes Servings: 2

Ingredients:
1 pound beef short ribs, trimmed of excess fat
Sea salt, to taste

Preheat your air fryer to 400°F (200°C) for 5 minutes.
Pat the beef short ribs dry with paper towels. Season generously with sea salt on all sides.
Place the short ribs in a single layer in the air fryer basket, ensuring they are not touching.
Air fry for 15-20 minutes, then flip the ribs and cook for another 15-20 minutes, or until they reach an internal temperature of 160°F (71°C) for medium-rare or 165°F (74°C) for medium.
Remove from the air fryer and let rest for 5 minutes before serving.

Nutritional Information (per serving):
Calories: 520
Fat: 45g
Protein: 40g
Carbs: 0g

Air Fryer Beef Liver

Prep Time: 5 minutes Cook Time: 12 minutes Total Time: 17 minutes Servings: 1

Ingredients:
1/2 pound beef liver, sliced into thin strips (about 1/4 inch thick)
Salt, to taste

Preheat your air fryer to 400°F (200°C).
Pat the beef liver dry with paper towels. Season generously with salt.
Arrange the liver strips in a single layer in the air fryer basket, making sure they are not touching.
Cook for 12 minutes, or until the liver is cooked through and slightly browned on the edges. Be careful not to overcook, as liver can become tough and dry quickly.
Check for doneness using an instant-read thermometer. The internal temperature should reach 165°F (74°C) for safe consumption.
Serve immediately.

Nutritional Information:
(per serving)
Calories: 230
Fat: 16g
Protein: 25g
Carbs: 0g
Sodium: 0mg (depending on how much salt you add)

Air Fryer Beef Tongue

Prep Time: 10 minutes Cooking Time: 30-40 minutes Total Time: 40-50 minutes Servings: 2

Ingredients:
1 pound beef tongue, trimmed and cleaned
Sea salt, to taste

Pre-cook the beef tongue: While not essential for air frying, pre-cooking the tongue ensures it cooks through evenly in the air fryer. Place the tongue in a pot, cover with water, and bring to a boil. Reduce heat, simmer for 2-3 hours, or until fork-tender. Remove from heat and let cool slightly.

Prepare the tongue for air frying: If pre-cooked, peel off the tough outer layer of skin. Slice the tongue into thin strips (around 1/4 inch thick). Pat dry with paper towels. Season generously with salt.

Air fry the tongue: Preheat your air fryer to 400°F (200°C). Arrange the tongue slices in a single layer in the air fryer basket, ensuring they don't overlap. Cook for 15-20 minutes, flipping halfway through, until golden brown and crispy on the edges.

Serve: Enjoy the air-fried beef tongue hot.

Nutritional Information (per serving):
Calories: 450-500
Protein: 60-65g
Fat: 30-35g
Carbs: 0g

PORK RECIPES
Air Fryer Pork Chops

Prep Time: 5 minutes Cook Time: 15-20 minutes Total Time: 20-25 minutes Servings: 2

Ingredients:
2 bone-in pork chops (about 1 inch thick)
Sea salt, to taste

Pat the pork chops dry with paper towels. Season generously with sea salt on both sides.
Preheat your air fryer to 400°F (200°C).
Place the pork chops in a single layer in the air fryer basket, ensuring they don't touch.
Cook for 10-12 minutes per side, or until the internal temperature reaches 145°F (63°C) for medium-rare or 160°F (71°C) for medium doneness, using a meat thermometer to check.
Remove from the air fryer and let rest for 5 minutes before serving.

Nutritional Information: (per serving)
Calories: 450-500
Fat: 35-40g
Protein: 30-35g
Carbs: 0g

Crispy Air Fried Pork Belly

Prep Time: 10 minutes Cook Time: 60-70 minutes Total Time: 70-80 minutes Servings: 2-3

Ingredients:
1 pound pork belly, skin on
1 tablespoon coarse sea salt

Score the skin: Using a sharp knife, carefully score the skin of the pork belly in a criss-cross pattern, making sure not to cut into the meat itself.
Season: Pat the pork belly dry with paper towels and rub the entire surface with coarse sea salt.
Air Fry: Preheat your air fryer to 320°F (160°C). Place the pork belly skin side up in the basket and air fry for 40 minutes.
Increase heat: After 40 minutes, increase the air fryer temperature to 400°F (200°C) and cook for an additional 20-30 minutes, or until the skin is puffed, golden brown, and crispy.
Rest and slice: Remove the pork belly from the air fryer and let it rest for 10 minutes before slicing. This allows the juices to redistribute for a more tender and flavorful pork belly.

Nutritional Information (per serving):
Calories: 500-600
Fat: 45-50g
Protein: 40-45g
Carbs: 0g

Garlic Parmesan Pork Bites

Prep Time: 5 minutes Cook Time: 15-20 minutes Total Time: 20-25 minutes Servings: 2

Ingredients:
1 pound boneless, skinless pork loin, cut into bite-sized pieces
2 tablespoons avocado oil
Sea salt, to taste
Freshly ground black pepper, to taste
2 tablespoons grated Parmesan cheese

Heat avocado oil in a large skillet over medium-high heat.
Season pork with salt and pepper.
Add pork to the hot skillet and cook for 5-7 minutes per side, or until browned and cooked through (internal temperature reaches 145°F).
Once cooked, remove pork from the skillet and set aside.
Reduce heat to low and add Parmesan cheese to the skillet. Cook for 1-2 minutes, stirring constantly, until cheese melts and becomes slightly golden brown.
Return the pork to the skillet and toss to coat with the melted cheese.
Serve immediately.

Nutritional Information:
Calories: 400 per serving
Protein: 50 grams per serving
Fat: 30 grams per serving
Carbs: 0 grams per serving

Cajun Spiced Pork Tenderloin

Prep Time: 5 minutes Cook Time: 25 minutes Total Time: 30 minutes Servings: 2

Ingredients:
1 pork tenderloin (1.5 - 2 lbs)
2 tablespoons Cajun seasoning
1/2 teaspoon coarse sea salt (optional)

Preheat oven to 425°F (220°C).
Pat the pork tenderloin dry with paper towels.
Season the pork generously with Cajun seasoning, rubbing it in evenly.
Place the pork tenderloin on a baking sheet or oven-safe skillet.
Roast for 20-25 minutes, or until the internal temperature reaches 145°F (63°C) for medium-rare, or 160°F (71°C) for well-done.
If desired, sprinkle with coarse sea salt before serving.
Let the pork rest for 5-10 minutes before slicing and serving.

Nutritional Information:
Calories: per serving 300-400 calories
Protein: 50-60 grams per serving
Fat: 20-30 grams per serving
Carbs: 0 grams per serving

Honey Mustard Glazed Pork Ribs

Prep Time: 10 minutes Cooking Time: 2-3 hours (depending on cooking method) Total Time: 2-3 hours and 10 minutes Servings: 4

Ingredients:
2 racks baby back pork ribs (about 3 lbs)
1/4 cup Dijon mustard
2 tablespoons apple cider vinegar
1 tablespoon raw honey
1/2 teaspoon black pepper

Preheat oven to 275°F (135°C).
Trim excess fat from the ribs, if desired.
In a small bowl, whisk together Dijon mustard, apple cider vinegar, honey, and black pepper.
Place the ribs on a baking sheet lined with parchment paper. Brush the ribs generously with the glaze on both sides.
Cover the baking sheet tightly with aluminum foil.
Bake for 2-2.5 hours, or until the meat is tender and starting to pull away from the bone.
Increase the oven temperature to broil. Broil the ribs for 3-5 minutes per side, or until golden brown and caramelized.
Let the ribs rest for 10 minutes before serving.

Nutritional Information (per serving):
Calories: 720
Fat: 58g
Protein: 70g
Carbs: 0g

Italian Herb Air Fryer Pork Loin

Prep Time: 5 minutes Cook Time: 30-35 minutes Total Time: 35-40 minutes Servings: 2-3

Ingredients:
1 pound boneless pork loin roast, trimmed of excess fat
1 teaspoon sea salt

Preheat your air fryer to 400°F (204°C) for 5 minutes.
Pat the pork loin dry with paper towels. Season generously with sea salt all over.
Place the pork loin in the air fryer basket, ensuring it doesn't touch the sides.
Cook for 20 minutes, then flip the pork loin and cook for an additional 10-15 minutes, or until the internal temperature reaches 145°F (63°C) measured with a meat thermometer.
Remove the pork loin from the air fryer and let it rest for 10 minutes before slicing.

Nutritional Information (per serving):
Calories: 450
Fat: 35g
Protein: 55g
Carbs: 0g

Teriyaki Pork Skewers

Prep Time: 10 minutes Cook Time: 15-20 minutes Total Time: 25-30 minutes Servings: 2

Ingredients:
1 pound pork tenderloin, cut into bite-sized pieces
1 tablespoon melted tallow or ghee
1/2 teaspoon sea salt
1/4 teaspoon black pepper
1/4 teaspoon garlic powder
1/4 teaspoon onion powder

Preheat your oven or grill to medium-high heat.
In a bowl, combine melted tallow, sea salt, black pepper, garlic powder, and onion powder.
Toss the pork pieces in the seasoning mixture to coat evenly.
Thread the pork pieces onto skewers.
Bake the skewers in the preheated oven for 15-20 minutes, or grill for 5-7 minutes per side, until cooked through and browned.

Nutritional Information (per serving):
Calories: 450-500
Fat: 40-45g
Protein: 40-45g
Carbs: 0g

Chili Lime Pork Carnitas

Prep Time: 10 minutes Cooking Time: 3-4 hours (depending on cooking method) Total Time: 3 hours 10 minutes (approximately) Servings: 4-6

Ingredients:
2 lbs pork shoulder (boneless, skinless)
Sea salt, to taste

Cut the pork shoulder into 2-inch cubes.
Generously season the pork with sea salt on all sides.
Choose your cooking method:
Slow Cooker: Place the pork cubes in a slow cooker and cook on low for 3-4 hours, or until the pork is very tender and easily shreds with a fork.
Oven: Preheat oven to 300°F (150°C). Place the pork cubes in a baking dish with a lid and cook for 3-4 hours, or until the pork is very tender and easily shreds with a fork.
Pressure Cooker: Follow your pressure cooker's instructions for cooking pork shoulder. This method will typically take around 1 hour.
Once cooked, remove the pork from the pot/oven and shred it with two forks.
Taste and adjust the salt level as desired.

Nutritional Information (per serving):
Calories: ~400-500 (depending on fat content of pork)
Protein: ~50-60 grams
Fat: ~30-40 grams
Carbs: 0 grams

Bacon-Wrapped Air Fryer Pork Tenderloin

Prep Time: 10 minutes Cook Time: 20-25 minutes Total Time: 30-35 minutes Servings: 2-3

Ingredients:
1 (1 ½ lb) pork tenderloin, trimmed and silver skin removed
5-6 slices thick-cut bacon
Salt
Pepper

Preheat your air fryer to 400°F (200°C) for 10 minutes.
Season the pork tenderloin generously with salt and pepper.
Lay the bacon slices flat, slightly overlapping, to form a wide band.
Place the seasoned pork tenderloin on the bacon and roll up tightly, jelly-roll style, starting with a long side.
Secure the roll with toothpicks if needed.
Lightly spray the air fryer basket with cooking spray (optional).
Place the bacon-wrapped pork tenderloin in the air fryer basket.
Cook for 20-25 minutes, or until the bacon is crispy and the internal temperature of the pork reaches 145°F (63°C) measured with a meat thermometer.
Remove the pork from the air fryer and let it rest for 5-10 minutes before slicing.

Nutritional Information: (per serving)
Calories: 450-500
Fat: 35-40g
Protein: 40-45g
Carbs: 0g

Spicy Sriracha Pork Wings

Prep Time: 10 minutes Cooking Time: 45-50 minutes Total Time: 55-60 minutes Servings: 2-3

Ingredients:
1 lb pork wings
1 tbsp sea salt
1 tbsp black pepper
1 tsp ground ginger
1/2 tsp garlic powder
1/4 tsp cayenne pepper (optional, for extra spice)
2 tbsp sriracha

Preheat oven to 400°F (200°C).
Pat the pork wings dry with paper towels.
In a bowl, combine sea salt, black pepper, ginger, garlic powder, and cayenne pepper (if using). Season the pork wings generously with the spice mixture.
Place the wings on a baking sheet in a single layer.
Bake for 30 minutes, then flip the wings and bake for an additional 15-20 minutes, or until cooked through and crispy.
In a small bowl, whisk together the sriracha.
Brush the sriracha sauce on the cooked wings during the last 5 minutes of baking for a sticky glaze, or toss in a bowl after baking.
Serve immediately.

Nutritional Information (per serving):
Calories: 450-500
Fat: 40-45g
Protein: 30-35g
Carbs: 0g

CHICKEN RECIPES

Carnivore Fried Chicken

Prep Time: 10 minutes Cook Time: 20 minutes Total Time: 30 minutes Servings: 2

Ingredients:
2 boneless, skinless chicken breasts or thighs
2 large eggs
1/2 cup pork rinds
1/2 teaspoon sea salt
1/4 teaspoon black pepper

Prep the chicken: Pat the chicken dry with paper towels. Cut them into strips or preferred serving sizes.
Make the breading: In a food processor, grind the pork rinds into a fine powder. Add the sea salt and black pepper, and pulse to combine.
Breading the chicken: Beat the eggs in a shallow bowl. Dip each piece of chicken in the egg mixture, ensuring full coverage. Dredge the chicken thoroughly in the pork rind mixture, pressing to coat evenly. Repeat the egg and pork rind coating process for a thicker crust (optional).
Air fry: Preheat your air fryer to 375°F (190°C). Lightly spray the air fryer basket with cooking oil (optional). Place the chicken pieces in a single layer, ensuring they don't touch.
Cook: Air fry for 12-15 minutes, or until the internal temperature of the chicken reaches 165°F (74°C). Flip the chicken halfway through for even cooking and crisping.
Serve: Enjoy your carnivore fried chicken hot and crispy!

Nutritional Information:
(Approximate values per serving)
Calories: 450
Fat: 35g
Protein: 40g
Carbs: 0g
Fiber: 0g

Air Fryer Keto Chicken Wings

Prep Time: 5 minutes Cook Time: 25-30 minutes Total Time: 30-35 minutes Servings: 2-3

Ingredients:
1 pound chicken wings
1 tablespoon avocado oil
1 teaspoon sea salt
1/2 teaspoon black pepper

Pat the chicken wings dry with paper towels.
In a bowl, toss the chicken wings with avocado oil, sea salt, and black pepper.
Preheat your air fryer to 400°F (204°C).
Arrange the chicken wings in a single layer in the air fryer basket, making sure they are not touching.
Cook for 20 minutes, then flip the wings and cook for an additional 5-10 minutes, or until the wings are cooked through and crispy. An internal temperature of 165°F (74°C) is recommended.
Serve immediately.

Nutritional Information (per serving):
Calories: 450
Fat: 40g
Protein: 30g
Carbs: 0g

Air Fryer Garlic Parmesan Chicken Thighs:

Prep Time: 5 minutes Cook Time: 20 minutes Total Time: 25 minutes Servings: 2

Ingredients:
2 bone-in, skin-on chicken thighs
1 tablespoon olive oil
1/2 teaspoon garlic powder
1/2 teaspoon sea salt

Pat the chicken thighs dry with paper towels.
Drizzle the chicken thighs with olive oil and coat them evenly with garlic powder and sea salt.
Preheat your air fryer to 400°F (204°C) for 5 minutes (if your air fryer has a preheat function).
Place the chicken thighs in a single layer in the air fryer basket, skin side up.
Cook for 20 minutes, or until the internal temperature of the thickest part of the chicken reaches 165°F (74°C).
Let the chicken rest for 5 minutes before serving.

Nutritional Information: (per serving)
Calories: 450
Fat: 35g
Protein: 45g
Carbs: 0g

Air Fryer Spicy Chicken Legs:

Prep Time: 10 minutes Cook Time: 25 minutes Total Time: 35 minutes Servings: 2

Ingredients:
2 bone-in, skin-on chicken legs
1 tablespoon olive oil
1/2 teaspoon chili powder
1/4 teaspoon smoked paprika
1/4 teaspoon garlic powder
1/4 teaspoon onion powder
1/8 teaspoon black pepper
Pinch of cayenne pepper (optional, for extra spice)

Preheat your air fryer to 400°F (200°C).
Pat the chicken legs dry with paper towels.
In a bowl, combine olive oil, chili powder, paprika, garlic powder, onion powder, black pepper, and cayenne pepper (if using).
Rub the spice mixture evenly onto the chicken legs, making sure to coat them well.
Place the chicken legs in a single layer in the air fryer basket, leaving space between them for even cooking.
Air fry for 20 minutes, then flip the chicken legs and cook for an additional 5 minutes, or until the internal temperature reaches 165°F (74°C) as measured with a meat thermometer.
Let the chicken legs rest for a few minutes before serving.

Nutritional Information (per serving):
Calories: 450
Fat: 35g
Protein: 40g
Carbs: 0g

Air Fryer Chicken Fajitas

Prep Time: 10 minutes Cook Time: 15 minutes Total Time: 25 minutes Servings: 2

Ingredients:
1 pound boneless, skinless chicken thighs, sliced into strips
1 tablespoon olive oil
1 tablespoon fajita seasoning (check label for non-carb ingredients)
Salt and pepper to taste

Preheat your air fryer to 400°F (204°C).
In a bowl, toss the chicken strips with olive oil, fajita seasoning, salt, and pepper.
Arrange the chicken strips in a single layer in the air fryer basket.
Cook for 12-15 minutes, or until the chicken is cooked through and golden brown, flipping halfway through.
Serve immediately with your favorite carnivore-compliant toppings, such as sliced avocado, salsa, or sour cream.

Nutritional Information (per serving):
Calories: 450
Fat: 35g
Protein: 45g
Carbs: 0g

Air Fryer Chicken Skewers

Prep Time: 10 minutes Cook Time: 15 minutes Total Time: 25 minutes Servings: 2

Ingredients:
1 pound boneless, skinless chicken thighs, cut into 1-inch pieces
1 tablespoon olive oil
1/2 teaspoon sea salt
1/4 teaspoon black pepper

Preheat your air fryer to 400°F (200°C).
In a bowl, toss the chicken pieces with olive oil, salt, and pepper.
Thread the chicken pieces onto skewers, leaving space between each piece for even cooking.
Place the skewers in a single layer in the air fryer basket.
Cook for 10-12 minutes, or until the chicken is cooked through and golden brown, flipping the skewers halfway through.
Serve immediately.

Nutritional Information (per serving):
Calories: 450
Fat: 35g
Protein: 40g
Carbs: 0g

Air Fryer Whole Chicken:

Prep Time: 10 minutes Cook Time: 45-60 minutes (depending on chicken size) Total Time: 55-70 minutes Servings: 4-6

Ingredients:
1 whole chicken (3-4 lbs)

Prep (10 minutes): Remove any giblets from the chicken cavity. Pat the chicken dry with paper towels.
Air Fry (45-60 minutes): Preheat your air fryer to 375°F (190°C). Place the chicken breast-side down in the basket. Cook for 30 minutes.
Flip and Cook (15-30 minutes): Carefully flip the chicken using tongs and cook for an additional 15-30 minutes, or until the internal temperature reaches 165°F (74°C) in the thickest part of the thigh.
Rest (10 minutes): Remove the chicken from the air fryer and let it rest on a cutting board for 10 minutes before carving and serving.

Nutritional Information: (per serving)
Calories: 450-550
Fat: 35-45g
Protein: 50-60g
Carbs: 0g

Air Fryer Chicken Nuggets:

Prep Time: 10 minutes Cook Time: 15 minutes Total Time: 25 minutes Servings: 2-3

Ingredients:
1 pound ground chicken
1/4 cup grated parmesan cheese
1/4 teaspoon garlic powder
1/4 teaspoon onion powder
Pinch of sea salt
Pinch of black pepper

In a large bowl, combine ground chicken, parmesan cheese, garlic powder, onion powder, salt, and pepper. Mix well to combine.
Form the mixture into small nuggets, about 1-inch in size.
Preheat your air fryer to 400°F (200°C).
Arrange the nuggets in a single layer in the air fryer basket, leaving space between them for even cooking.
Cook for 10-12 minutes, or until golden brown and cooked through. Depending on your air fryer, you may need to flip the nuggets halfway through cooking.
Serve immediately with your favorite dipping sauce (optional, ensure it complies with the carnivore diet).

Nutritional Information: (per serving)
Calories: 350
Fat: 25g
Protein: 40g
Carbs: 0g

Air Fryer Chicken Tenders

Prep Time: 5 minutes Cook Time: 15 minutes Total Time: 20 minutes Servings: 2

Ingredients:
1 pound boneless, skinless chicken tenders
1 tablespoon olive oil or avocado oil
1/2 teaspoon sea salt
1/4 teaspoon black pepper
1/4 teaspoon garlic powder
1/4 teaspoon onion powder

Preheat your air fryer to 400°F (200°C).
Pat the chicken tenders dry with paper towels.
In a bowl, toss the chicken tenders with olive oil, salt, pepper, garlic powder, and onion powder.
Arrange the chicken tenders in a single layer in the air fryer basket, ensuring they don't touch.
Air fry for 12-15 minutes, or until the chicken is cooked through and golden brown. Flip the tenders halfway through cooking for even browning.
Check the internal temperature of the thickest part of the chicken tenders with a meat thermometer. It should reach 165°F (74°C) for safe consumption.
Serve immediately and enjoy!

Nutritional Information:
(per serving)
Calories: 350
Fat: 25g
Protein: 40g
Carbs: 0g
Fiber: 0g
Sodium: 350mg

Air Fryer Buffalo Chicken Wings

Prep Time: 10 minutes Cook Time: 26 minutes Total Time: 36 minutes Servings: 2-3

Ingredients:
1.5 pounds chicken wings (drumettes and flats preferred)
1/4 cup melted butter
1/4 cup hot sauce (such as Frank's RedHot)
1/4 teaspoon salt
1/4 teaspoon black pepper

Pat the chicken wings dry with paper towels.
In a small bowl, whisk together the melted butter, hot sauce, salt, and pepper.
Place the chicken wings in a single layer in the air fryer basket.
Air fry at 400°F (200°C) for 20 minutes, flipping the wings halfway through.
Once the wings are cooked through and crispy, remove them from the air fryer and toss them in the buffalo sauce mixture.
Serve immediately with your favorite dipping sauce, such as blue cheese or ranch dressing (optional, not part of the carnivore diet).

Nutritional Information (per serving):
Calories: 450
Fat: 35g
Protein: 40g
Carbs: 0g

Air Fryer BBQ Chicken:

Prep Time: 5 minutes Cook Time: 20-25 minutes Total Time: 25-30 minutes Servings: 2

Ingredients:
2 boneless, skinless chicken breasts
1/2 teaspoon sea salt

Preheat your air fryer to 400°F (200°C).
Pat the chicken breasts dry with paper towels. Season both sides with sea salt.
Place the chicken breasts in a single layer in the air fryer basket.
Cook for 10-12 minutes per side, or until the internal temperature reaches 165°F (74°C) using a meat thermometer.
Remove from the air fryer and let rest for 5 minutes before serving.

Nutritional Information:
(per serving)
Calories: 250
Fat: 12g
Protein: 30g
Carbs: 0g

LAMB RECIPES

Pan-Seared Lamb Chops with Garlic Butter

Prep Time: 5 minutes Cook Time: 10-12 minutes Total Time: 15 minutes Servings: 2

Ingredients:
2 bone-in lamb chops
2 tablespoons unsalted butter
2 cloves garlic, minced
Sea salt
Freshly ground black pepper

Pat the lamb chops dry with paper towels. Season generously with salt and pepper.
Heat a cast iron skillet over medium-high heat until very hot. Sear the lamb chops for 3-4 minutes per side, or until desired doneness is reached.
While the lamb chops are searing, melt the butter in a small pan over medium heat. Add the garlic and cook for 30 seconds, until fragrant. Be careful not to burn the garlic.
Remove the lamb chops from the pan and let them rest for 5 minutes before serving. Spoon the garlic butter over the lamb chops and enjoy.

Nutritional Information (per serving):
Calories: 450
Fat: 35g
Protein: 40g
Carbs: 0g

Keto Lamb Kofta

Prep Time: 10 minutes Cook Time: 15 minutes Total Time: 25 minutes Servings: 4

Ingredients:
1 pound ground lamb
2 cloves garlic, minced
1 tablespoon dried oregano
1/2 teaspoon ground cumin
1/4 teaspoon sea salt
1/4 teaspoon black pepper

In a large bowl, combine the ground lamb, garlic, oregano, cumin, salt, and pepper. Mix well with your hands until everything is evenly incorporated.
Form the mixture into 8 equal-sized koftas. You can shape them into oblong patties or round meatballs.
Heat a cast iron skillet or grill pan over medium-high heat. Once hot, add the koftas and cook for 5-7 minutes per side, or until browned and cooked through.
Serve immediately.

Nutritional Information:
Calories: 350
Fat: 28g
Protein: 30g
Carbs: 0g
Net Carbs: 0g

Air Fryer Lamb Merguez Sausage:

Prep Time: 5 minutes Cook Time: 10-12 minutes Total Time: 15-17 minutes Servings: 2

Ingredients:
6 oz lamb merguez sausages (casing removed, optional)
Salt and pepper to taste

Preheat: Preheat your air fryer to 400°F (200°C) for 5 minutes.
Season: If using casings, poke the sausages a few times with a fork. Season generously with salt and pepper.
Air Fry: Place the sausages in a single layer in the air fryer basket, ensuring they don't touch. Cook for 10-12 minutes, flipping halfway through, until the sausages are browned and cooked through.
Serve: Enjoy hot!

Nutritional Information (per serving):
Calories: 430
Fat: 38g
Protein: 25g
Carbs: 0g

Air Fryer Lamb Kebabs

Prep Time: 10 minutes Cook Time: 15 minutes Total Time: 25 minutes Servings: 2

Ingredients:
1/2 pound ground lamb
1 tablespoon olive oil
1/2 teaspoon dried oregano
1/4 teaspoon garlic powder
1/4 teaspoon smoked paprika
Salt and pepper to taste
2 metal skewers

In a bowl, combine lamb, olive oil, oregano, garlic powder, paprika, salt, and pepper. Mix well to coat the lamb evenly.

Thread the lamb mixture onto the skewers, forming evenly sized kebabs.

Preheat your air fryer to 400°F (200°C).

Place the kebabs in the air fryer basket, ensuring they aren't touching.

Cook for 10-12 minutes, or until the lamb is cooked through and slightly browned on the outside.

Flip the kebabs halfway through cooking for even browning.

Serve hot with your desired dipping sauce.

Nutritional Information (per serving):
Calories: 430
Fat: 32g
Protein: 30g
Carbs: 0g

Air Fryer Ground Lamb Burgers

Prep Time: 5 minutes Cook Time: 15 minutes Total Time: 20 minutes Servings: 2

Ingredients:
1 pound ground lamb
1 teaspoon dried oregano
1/2 teaspoon garlic powder
1/2 teaspoon onion powder
1/4 teaspoon black pepper
Salt to taste

In a medium bowl, combine ground lamb, oregano, garlic powder, onion powder, pepper, and salt. Mix gently until just combined.
Divide the mixture into two equal portions and shape them into patties.
Preheat your air fryer to 375°F (190°C) for 3-5 minutes.
Place the lamb burger patties in a single layer in the air fryer basket, ensuring they don't touch.
Cook for 7-8 minutes, then flip the patties and cook for an additional 7-8 minutes, or until the internal temperature reaches 160°F (71°C) for medium-rare.
Remove the burgers from the air fryer and let them rest for 5 minutes before serving.

Nutritional Information (per serving):
Calories: 480
Fat: 38g
Protein: 40g
Carbs: 0g

Air Fryer Lamb Sliders:

Prep Time: 10 minutes Cook Time: 12 minutes Total Time: 22 minutes Servings: 4

Ingredients:
1 pound ground lamb
1/4 teaspoon dried oregano
1/4 teaspoon garlic powder
1/4 teaspoon onion powder
1/4 teaspoon smoked paprika
Salt and pepper to taste
4 slider buns (optional, for those not strictly following carnivore)

In a medium bowl, combine ground lamb, oregano, garlic powder, onion powder, smoked paprika, salt, and pepper. Mix well to combine without overworking the meat.

Shape the lamb mixture into 4 equal patties, slightly smaller than your slider buns.

Preheat your air fryer to 400°F (200°C) for 3-5 minutes.

Place the lamb patties in a single layer in the air fryer basket, ensuring they don't touch.

Cook for 6 minutes per side, or until the internal temperature reaches 160°F (71°C) for medium-rare or 165°F (74°C) for well done.

While the lamb cooks, toast the slider buns in the air fryer (optional), cut-side down, for 2-3 minutes, or until lightly golden brown.

Serve the lamb patties on the toasted buns (optional) and enjoy!

Nutritional Information (per serving without buns):
Calories: 420
Fat: 34g
Protein: 32g
Carbs: 0g
Fiber: 0g

Air Fryer Lamb Gyro Meat:

Prep Time: 10 minutes Cook Time: 10-15 minutes Total Time: 20-25 minutes Servings: 2

Ingredients:
1 pound ground lamb
1/2 teaspoon dried oregano
1/4 teaspoon dried basil
1/2 teaspoon onion powder
1/4 teaspoon garlic powder
1/4 teaspoon dried thyme
1/4 teaspoon ground fennel seed
1/4 teaspoon paprika
1/4 teaspoon black pepper

In a small bowl, combine lamb, oregano, basil, onion powder, garlic powder, thyme, fennel seed, paprika, and black pepper. Mix well.

Form the lamb mixture into two 2-inch thick patties.

Preheat your air fryer to 375°F (190°C).

Place the patties in your air fryer basket, ensuring they don't touch.

Cook for 8-10 minutes, then flip the patties and continue cooking for another 5-7 minutes, or until the internal temperature reaches 160°F (71°C) for medium-well doneness.

Remove from the air fryer and let rest for a few minutes before serving.

Nutritional Information (per serving):
Calories: 480
Fat: 35g
Protein: 45g
Carbs: 0g

Air Fryer Lamb Chops with Bacon

Prep Time: 5 minutes Cook Time: 15-20 minutes Total Time: 20-25 minutes Servings: 2

Ingredients:
2 bone-in lamb chops (about 1/2 inch thick)
4 slices thick-cut bacon
Salt and pepper to taste

Preheat your air fryer to 400°F (200°C).
Pat the lamb chops dry with paper towels. Season generously with salt and pepper.
Wrap each lamb chop with 2 slices of bacon, securing the ends with toothpicks if needed.
Place the lamb chops in a single layer in the air fryer basket, ensuring they don't touch.
Cook for 15-20 minutes, or until the bacon is crispy and the lamb reaches your desired doneness (145°F for medium-rare, 160°F for medium). Use a meat thermometer to check the internal temperature.
Let the lamb chops rest for 5 minutes before serving.

Nutritional Information (per serving):
Calories: 550-600
Fat: 45-50g
Protein: 40-45g
Carbs: 0g

Air Fryer Lamb Kofta Kebabs

Prep Time: 15 minutes Cook Time: 10 minutes Total Time: 25 minutes Servings: 2

Ingredients:
1/2 pound ground lamb
1/4 cup chopped onion
1 tablespoon chopped fresh parsley
1/2 teaspoon ground cumin
1/4 teaspoon chili powder
1/4 teaspoon garlic powder
Salt and pepper to taste

In a large bowl, combine the lamb, onion, parsley, cumin, chili powder, garlic powder, salt, and pepper. Mix well to combine.
Form the lamb mixture into small, sausage-shaped kebabs.
Preheat your air fryer to 400°F (200°C).
Place the kebabs in a single layer in the air fryer basket and cook for 10 minutes, or until cooked through.
Serve immediately with your favorite dipping sauce, such as chimichurri or tzatziki.

Nutritional Information: (per serving)
Calories: 350
Fat: 25g
Protein: 30g
Carbs: 0g

SEAFOOD RECIPES
Air Fryer Garlic Herb Salmon

Prep Time: 5 minutes Cook Time: 10-12 minutes Total Time: 15 minutes Servings: 2

Ingredients:
2 salmon fillets (6 oz/170g each), skin and bones removed
1 tablespoon melted butter or ghee
1 clove garlic, minced (optional, for a more intense flavor)
1/2 teaspoon dried thyme
1/4 teaspoon dried oregano
Salt and pepper to taste

Preheat your air fryer to 400°F (200°C).
Pat the salmon fillets dry with paper towels. Season both sides with salt and pepper.
In a small bowl, combine melted butter or ghee, garlic (if using), thyme, and oregano.
Brush the salmon fillets with the herb butter mixture.
Place the salmon fillets in the air fryer basket, skin-side down (if applicable). If your air fryer doesn't have a basket, you can place the salmon on a baking sheet lined with parchment paper.
Air fry for 10-12 minutes, or until the salmon is cooked through and flakes easily with a fork. The internal temperature of the salmon should reach 145°F (63°C) for medium-rare or 160°F (71°C) for well-done.

Nutritional Information (per serving):
Calories: 450-500
Fat: 35-40g
Protein: 40-45g
Carbs: 0g

Air Fryer Parmesan Crusted Tilapia

Prep Time: 5 minutes Cook Time: 7-8 minutes Total Time: 12-13 minutes Servings: 2

Ingredients:
2 Tilapia fillets
1/2 cup grated Parmesan cheese
1 teaspoon garlic powder
1/2 teaspoon black pepper
Cooking spray

Preheat your air fryer to 400°F (200°C).

Pat the tilapia fillets dry with paper towels.

In a shallow bowl, combine the Parmesan cheese, garlic powder, and black pepper.

Lightly spray the tilapia fillets with cooking spray.

Dredge each fillet in the parmesan mixture, pressing gently to coat evenly.

Place the breaded tilapia in a single layer in the air fryer basket, ensuring they don't touch.

Cook for 7-8 minutes, or until the fish is golden brown and flakes easily with a fork.

Nutritional Information: (per serving)
Calories: 230
Fat: 13g
Protein: 30g
Carbs: 0g

Air Fryer Cajun Shrimp

Prep Time: 5 minutes Cook Time: 8 minutes Total Time: 13 minutes Servings: 1

Ingredients:
1 pound large shrimp, peeled and deveined
1 tablespoon olive oil
1 tablespoon Cajun seasoning (check the label to ensure it is carnivore-compliant, meaning no added sugars or starches)

Pat the shrimp dry with paper towels.
In a bowl, toss the shrimp with olive oil and Cajun seasoning until evenly coated.
Preheat your air fryer to 400°F (200°C).
Arrange the shrimp in a single layer in the air fryer basket, ensuring they are not touching.
Cook for 4 minutes, then shake the basket and cook for an additional 4 minutes, or until the shrimp are pink and opaque throughout.

Nutritional Information:
(Based on 1 pound of shrimp and 1 tablespoon of olive oil)
Calories: 430
Fat: 31g
Protein: 45g
Carbs: 0g

Air Fryer Lobster Tails with Garlic Butter

Prep Time: 5 minutes Cook Time: 5-7 minutes Total Time: 10-12 minutes Servings: 2

Ingredients:
2 fresh lobster tails (thawed if frozen)
2 tablespoons unsalted butter, melted
2 cloves garlic, minced
Salt and pepper to taste

Prepare the lobster tails: Using kitchen shears, butterfly the lobster tails by cutting down the center through the top shell and meat. Be careful not to cut all the way through the bottom. Open the lobster tails flat and remove any visible veins.

Make the garlic butter: In a small bowl, combine the melted butter and minced garlic. Season with salt and pepper to taste.

Preheat the air fryer: Preheat your air fryer to 380°F (195°C).

Season and coat the lobster: Brush the lobster meat generously with the garlic butter mixture. Season with additional salt and pepper, if desired.

Air fry the lobster: Place the lobster tails in the air fryer basket, with the meat facing up. Cook for 5-7 minutes, or until the flesh is opaque and slightly browned.

Serve: Enjoy the lobster tails immediately, drizzled with any remaining garlic butter sauce.

Nutritional Information (per serving):
Calories: 340
Fat: 28g
Protein: 42g
Carbs: 0g

Air Fryer Scallops with Lemon and Herbs

Prep Time: 5 minutes Cook Time: 6-8 minutes Total Time: 11-13 minutes Servings: 2

Ingredients:
8 large sea scallops (cleaned and patted dry)
1 tablespoon olive oil
1/2 teaspoon dried parsley
1/4 teaspoon dried thyme
1/4 teaspoon garlic powder
Salt and pepper to taste

In a small bowl, combine olive oil, parsley, thyme, garlic powder, salt, and pepper.
Toss the scallops in the herb mixture to coat evenly.
Preheat your air fryer to 400°F (200°C).
Arrange the scallops in a single layer in the air fryer basket, ensuring they don't touch.
Cook for 3-4 minutes per side, or until opaque and cooked through. Be careful not to overcook, as scallops become tough quickly.
Serve immediately.

Nutritional Information (per serving):
Calories: 220
Fat: 15g
Protein: 20g
Carbs: 0g

Air Fryer Calamari with Marinara Sauce

Prep Time: 10 minutes Cook Time: 10 minutes Total Time: 20 minutes Servings: 2

Ingredients:
8 oz squid rings, cleaned and patted dry
1 large egg, beaten
1/4 cup pork rinds, crushed
1 tsp garlic powder
1/2 tsp onion powder
1/4 tsp black pepper
Marinara sauce for serving (optional, choose a sugar-free option)

Preheat your air fryer to 400°F (200°C) for 5 minutes.
In a shallow bowl, whisk together the beaten egg.
In another shallow bowl, combine the crushed pork rinds, garlic powder, onion powder, and black pepper.
Dip each squid ring in the egg mixture, then coat evenly in the pork rind mixture.
Arrange the breaded calamari in a single layer in your air fryer basket, ensuring they don't touch.
Air fry for 8-10 minutes, or until golden brown and crispy, flipping halfway through.
Serve immediately with your preferred sugar-free marinara sauce for dipping, if desired.

Nutritional Information: (per serving)
Calories: 350
Fat: 25 g
Protein: 40 g
Carbs: 0 g
Net Carbs: 0 g

Air Fryer Fish Sticks

Prep Time: 10 minutes Cook Time: 10 minutes Total Time: 20 minutes Servings: 2

Ingredients:
1 pound white fish (cod, haddock, or tilapia) cut into sticks
1/4 cup mayonnaise
1 tablespoon Dijon mustard
1 tablespoon water
1 cup pork rinds, crushed
1/2 teaspoon paprika
1/4 teaspoon garlic powder
Salt and pepper to taste

In a shallow bowl, whisk together the mayonnaise, Dijon mustard, and water.
In another shallow bowl, combine the crushed pork rinds, paprika, garlic powder, salt, and pepper.
Dip each fish stick in the mayo mixture, letting any excess drip off.
Roll the fish stick in the pork rind mixture, coating it completely.
Preheat your air fryer to 400°F (200°C).
Arrange the fish sticks in a single layer in the air fryer basket, making sure they are not touching.
Air fry for 10 minutes, or until golden brown and flaky.
Serve immediately with your favorite dipping sauce.

Nutritional Information (per serving):
Calories: 450
Fat: 35g
Protein: 40g
Carbs: 0g

Air Fryer Crab Cakes

Prep Time: 10 minutes Cook Time: 12 minutes Total Time: 22 minutes Servings: 4

Ingredients:
1 pound lump crabmeat, picked over for shells and cartilage
2 large eggs, beaten
1/4 cup mayonnaise
1 tablespoon chopped fresh parsley
1 tablespoon chopped fresh chives
1 teaspoon Old Bay seasoning
1/2 teaspoon black pepper
Avocado oil spray

In a large bowl, combine the crabmeat, eggs, mayonnaise, parsley, chives, Old Bay seasoning, and black pepper. Mix gently to combine without breaking up the crabmeat too much.
Form the mixture into 4 equal patties, about 3-4 inches in diameter and 1 inch thick.
Preheat your air fryer to 400°F (200°C). Lightly spray the air fryer basket with avocado oil spray.
Place the crab cakes in the air fryer basket, ensuring they don't touch. Spray the tops of the crab cakes with avocado oil spray.
Cook for 10 minutes, then carefully flip the crab cakes and cook for an additional 2 minutes, or until golden brown and cooked through.
Serve immediately with lemon wedges and your favorite dipping sauce, if desired.

Nutritional Information (per serving):
Calories: 450
Fat: 35g
Protein: 40g
Carbs: 0g

Air Fryer Oysters Rockefeller

Prep Time: 10 minutes Cook Time: 10 minutes Total Time: 20 minutes Servings: 2

Ingredients:
12 fresh oysters on the half shell
2 tbsp chopped fresh spinach
1 tbsp chopped fresh parsley
1 tbsp chopped chives
1 tbsp melted ghee or avocado oil
1/4 tsp garlic powder
1/4 tsp onion powder
Pinch of sea salt
Pinch of black pepper

Preheat your air fryer to 400°F (204°C).

In a small bowl, combine the spinach, parsley, chives, ghee, garlic powder, onion powder, salt, and pepper. Shuck the oysters, taking care not to spill any of the liquor. Discard the top shell and arrange the oysters in a single layer on a baking sheet lined with parchment paper.

Divide the spinach mixture evenly among the oysters.

Place the baking sheet in the air fryer basket and cook for 8-10 minutes, or until the topping is golden brown and the oysters are cooked through.

Be careful when removing the oysters as they will be hot. Serve immediately.

Nutritional Information (per serving):
Calories: 140
Fat: 10g
Protein: 12g
Carbs: 3g
Fiber: 1g

Air Fryer Spicy Tuna Steaks

Prep Time: 5 minutes Cook Time: 4-6 minutes Total Time: 9-11 minutes Servings: 1

Ingredients:
1 (6-ounce) ahi tuna steak
1 tablespoon olive oil
1/2 teaspoon chili powder
1/4 teaspoon smoked paprika
1/4 teaspoon garlic powder
1/4 teaspoon black pepper
Pinch of cayenne pepper (optional)

Preheat your air fryer to 400°F (200°C).
Pat the tuna steak dry with paper towels.
In a small bowl, combine the olive oil, chili powder, smoked paprika, garlic powder, black pepper, and cayenne pepper (if using).
Rub the spice mixture evenly over both sides of the tuna steak.
Place the tuna steak in a single layer in the air fryer basket.
Cook for 4-5 minutes for rare, 5-6 minutes for medium-rare, or 6-7 minutes for medium-done.
Carefully remove the tuna steak from the air fryer and let it rest for 2-3 minutes before slicing and serving.

Nutritional Information (per serving):
Calories: 450
Fat: 35g
Protein: 50g
Carbs: 0g

GAME RECIPES

Seared Bison Steak with Herb Butter

Prep Time: 5 minutes Cook Time: 10-12 minutes (depending on desired doneness) Total Time: 15-17 minutes Servings: 1

Ingredients:
1 (8oz) thick-cut bison steak
1 tbsp unsalted butter, softened
1/2 tsp fresh rosemary, chopped
1/4 tsp fresh thyme, chopped
Salt and freshly ground black pepper to taste

Make herb butter: In a small bowl, combine softened butter, rosemary, thyme, and a pinch of salt and pepper. Mix well and set aside.
Season steak: Pat the bison steak dry and season generously with salt and pepper.
Heat a cast iron skillet over medium-high heat. Once hot, add the steak and sear for 3-4 minutes per side for medium-rare, or longer for desired doneness.
Reduce heat: Once seared, lower the heat to medium and add a pat of herb butter to the pan. Tilt the pan slightly and spoon the melted butter over the steak for about 30 seconds to baste.
Transfer steak to a plate and let it rest for 5 minutes before slicing. Top with remaining herb butter and serve.

Nutritional Information: (approximate values per serving)
Calories: 520
Fat: 42g
Protein: 50g
Carbs: 0g

Burger Bowls

Prep Time: 10 minutes Cooking Time: 15 minutes Total Time: 25 minutes Servings: 2

Ingredients:
1 lb ground beef (or other carnivore-approved ground meat)
1 tbsp olive oil or avocado oil
1/2 tsp onion powder
1/4 tsp garlic powder
1/4 tsp smoked paprika
Salt and freshly ground black pepper to taste
4 oz sliced mushrooms (optional, for added texture)
Chopped fresh herbs like parsley or chives (optional, for garnish)

Heat oil in a large skillet over medium-high heat.
Add ground meat and spices: Crumble the meat into the pan and season with onion powder, garlic powder, smoked paprika, salt, and pepper. Cook, breaking up the meat with a spatula, until browned and cooked through.
Add mushrooms (optional): If using, add the sliced mushrooms to the pan and cook until softened, about 5 minutes.
Assemble bowls: Divide the cooked meat mixture between two bowls. Top with desired toppings like chopped raw onions, sliced avocado, or your favorite carnivore-approved sauces.
Garnish with fresh herbs (optional) and serve.

Nutritional Information: (approximate values per serving)
Calories: 580
Fat: 45g
Protein: 55g
Carbs: 0g

Meatballs with Creamy Sauce

Prep Time: 15 minutes Cook Time: 20 minutes Total Time: 35 minutes Servings: 4

Ingredients:
For the meatballs:
1 lb ground pork (or other carnivore-approved ground meat)
1/2 cup grated hard cheese (optional, some carnivore variations allow small amounts of dairy)
1 egg
1/4 cup chopped onion (optional, for added flavor)
1 tsp dried thyme
1/2 tsp salt
1/4 tsp black pepper

For the creamy sauce:
1 tbsp olive oil or avocado oil
1/2 cup chopped onion (optional)
1/4 cup heavy cream (or full-fat coconut milk for a dairy-free option)
1/4 cup bone broth
1 tsp dried rosemary
1/2 tsp salt
1/4 tsp black pepper

Preheat oven to 400°F (200°C).

Combine meatball ingredients: In a large bowl, combine ground meat, cheese (if using), egg, onion (if using), thyme, salt, and pepper. Mix well using your hands until evenly combined.

Form meatballs: Roll the mixture into 1-inch balls and place them on a baking sheet lined with parchment paper.

Bake meatballs: Bake for 15-20 minutes, or until cooked through and golden brown.

While meatballs are baking, prepare the sauce: In a saucepan over medium heat, heat olive oil. Add onion (if using) and cook until softened, about 5 minutes.

Whisk in remaining sauce ingredients: Add heavy cream or coconut milk, bone broth, rosemary, salt, and pepper. Bring to a simmer and cook for 5 minutes, or until slightly thickened.

Transfer cooked meatballs to the sauce: Once the sauce is thickened, gently transfer the meatballs to the pan and coat them in the sauce.

Simmer for a few minutes: Let the meatballs simmer for an additional 2-3 minutes to allow the flavors to meld.

Serve hot: Enjoy the meatballs with the creamy sauce, garnished with fresh herbs like parsley (optional).

Nutritional Information: (approximate values per serving)
Calories: 450
Fat: 35g
Protein: 30g
Carbs: 2g (from onions, if used)

Meat Skewers with Chimichurri

Prep Time: 15 minutes Marinating Time: (optional) 30 minutes to 2 hours Cooking Time: 10-12 minutes Total Time: 25-35 minutes (depending on marinating) Servings: 2

Ingredients:
For the skewers:
1 lb boneless, skinless "game" meat cut into bite-sized pieces (such as ostrich steak, venison tenderloin, or bison flank steak)
1 tbsp olive oil or avocado oil
1/2 tsp salt
1/4 tsp black pepper
For the chimichurri:
1/4 cup fresh parsley, chopped
1/4 cup fresh cilantro, chopped
1 tbsp fresh oregano, chopped (or 1/2 tsp dried)
1 tbsp olive oil
1 tbsp red wine vinegar
1 clove garlic, minced
1/4 tsp salt
1/4 tsp red pepper flakes (optional)

Marinate the meat (optional): In a bowl, combine the meat, olive oil, salt, and pepper. Toss to coat and refrigerate for at least 30 minutes or up to 2 hours.
Prepare the chimichurri: Combine all chimichurri ingredients in a small bowl and mix well. Set aside.
Preheat grill or grill pan: Preheat your grill or grill pan to medium-high heat.
Assemble skewers: Thread the marinated meat pieces onto metal skewers. If not marinating, simply thread the meat onto skewers and season with additional salt and pepper.
Grill the skewers: Grill the skewers for 3-4 minutes per side, or until cooked through to your desired doneness.
Serve with chimichurri: Transfer the cooked skewers to a plate and enjoy them hot with the chimichurri sauce for dipping.

Nutritional Information: (approximate values per serving)
Calories: 480
Fat: 40g
Protein: 50g
Carbs: 0g

Breakfast Scramble

Prep Time: 5 minutes Cook Time: 10 minutes Total Time: 15 minutes Servings: 1

Ingredients:
2 eggs
1/4 cup ground "game" meat (such as bison, elk, or ostrich)
1/4 cup chopped mushrooms (optional)
1 tbsp chopped onion (optional)
1/4 cup shredded cheese (optional, some carnivore variations allow small amounts of dairy)
Salt and pepper to taste

Heat a non-stick pan over medium heat.
Sauté onion and mushrooms (optional): If using, add the onion and mushrooms to the pan and cook until softened, about 5 minutes.
Add ground meat: Crumble the ground meat into the pan and cook until browned and cooked through, breaking it up with a spatula.
Whisk the eggs: In a bowl, whisk the eggs with salt and pepper.
Pour eggs into the pan: Once the meat is cooked, pour the whisked eggs into the pan, allowing them to spread around the meat and vegetables.
Scramble the eggs: Use a spatula to gently fold and scramble the eggs until they are cooked through to your desired consistency.
Top with cheese (optional): If using, sprinkle the shredded cheese over the cooked scramble and let it melt for a few seconds.
Serve hot: Enjoy the scramble immediately.

Nutritional Information: (approximate values per serving)
Calories: 380
Fat: 30g
Protein: 25g
Carbs: 1g (from onions, if used)

Meat Jerky

Prep Time: 10 minutes Marinating Time: 12-24 hours (recommended) Drying Time: 6-8 hours (depending on thickness) Total Time: 18-32 hours (depending on marinating) Yield: Varies depending on the amount of meat used

Ingredients:
1 lb lean "game" meat (such as venison, elk, or bison) sliced very thin (against the grain)
1 tbsp sea salt
1 tsp black pepper
Optional additions: garlic powder, onion powder, smoked paprika, cayenne pepper (to taste)

Directions:
Freeze the meat: Flash freeze the sliced meat for about 30 minutes to firm it up, making it easier to slice thin.
Marinate (optional): In a non-reactive bowl (like glass or stainless steel), combine the sliced meat, salt, pepper, and any additional spices you are using. Mix well and cover. Refrigerate for at least 12 hours, or up to 24 hours, for deeper flavor.
Prepare your dehydrator: Set your dehydrator to 160°F (71°C). Arrange the marinated meat slices in a single layer on the dehydrator trays, ensuring they don't touch.
Dehydrate the meat: Dry the meat for 6-8 hours, or until it is completely dry and leathery to the touch. The drying time can vary depending on the thickness of the meat slices and your dehydrator's specific settings.
Test for dryness: Bend a piece of jerky. If it cracks but doesn't break, it's done. If it's still flexible, it needs more drying time.
Cool and store: Once the jerky is completely dry, let it cool completely at room temperature. Store the jerky in an airtight container in a cool, dry place for up to 2 weeks.

Tips:
Use lean cuts of meat for best results.
Marinating is optional, but it adds flavor and helps tenderize the meat.
Be sure to slice the meat very thin against the grain for faster and more even drying.
Check on the jerky periodically during the drying process to ensure it's drying properly and not burning.
You can adjust the amount of spices and seasonings to your preference.

SIDE DISHES
Crispy Bacon

Prep Time: 2 minutes Cook Time: 15-20 minutes Total Time: 17-22 minutes Servings: 1

Ingredients:
2-3 slices uncured bacon (choose thick-cut for extra crispiness)

Preheat oven to 400°F (200°C).
Line a baking sheet with parchment paper for easier cleanup (optional).
Lay the bacon strips flat on the prepared baking sheet in a single layer, making sure they don't overlap.
Bake for 15-20 minutes, or until the bacon is golden brown and crispy, flipping halfway through.
Remove from the oven and let cool slightly before serving.

Nutritional Information (per serving):
Calories: 180-240
Fat: 14-18g
Protein: 8-10g
Carbs: 0g

Air Fryer Sausage Links

Prep Time: 5 minutes Cook Time: 10-12 minutes Total Time: 15-17 minutes Servings: 2

Ingredients:
4 high-quality pork sausage links (casing removed, optional)
1 tablespoon avocado oil (optional)

Preheat your air fryer to 400°F (204°C).
If using, toss the sausage links in avocado oil to lightly coat them.
Arrange the sausage links in a single layer in the air fryer basket, ensuring they are not touching.
Air fry for 10-12 minutes, or until golden brown and cooked through (internal temperature should reach 160°F (71°C)).
Flip the sausages halfway through cooking for even browning.
Remove from the air fryer and let cool slightly before serving.

Nutritional Information: (per serving)
Calories: 350-400 (depending on the sausage)
Fat: 30-35g
Protein: 20-25g
Carbs: 0g

Beef Jerky

Prep Time: 30 minutes Dehydrating Time: 6-8 hours (depending on thickness and desired texture) Total Time: 6.5-8.5 hours Servings: 10-12 (depending on desired serving size)

Ingredients:
2 pounds lean beef (flank steak, top round, or bottom round)
1/4 cup sea salt (coarse or kosher)

Slice the beef: Freeze the beef for 30 minutes to make it easier to slice thinly against the grain. Using a sharp knife, slice the beef into strips about 1/4 inch thick.

Salt the beef: Place the beef strips in a large bowl and toss with the sea salt. Ensure all surfaces are evenly coated.

Marinate (optional): While not strictly necessary for the carnivore diet, you can marinate the beef for 30 minutes to 2 hours in the refrigerator for additional flavor. However, only use water or other carnivore-compliant ingredients like apple cider vinegar.

Dehydrate: Arrange the beef strips in a single layer on dehydrator trays, ensuring no pieces are touching. Set the dehydrator to 165°F (74°C) and dehydrate for 6-8 hours, or until the jerky is dry and leathery but still slightly pliable. You can bend the jerky without it breaking.

Test and cool: Once the jerky is dry, remove it from the dehydrator and let it cool completely for at least 30 minutes. During this time, the jerky will continue to firm up slightly.

Store: Store the jerky in an airtight container in a cool, dry place for up to 2 weeks.

Nutritional Information (per 1 oz serving):
Calories: 110
Fat: 7g
Protein: 17g
Carbs: 0g
Sodium: 400mg (depending on the salt content)

Pork Rinds

Prep Time: 5 minutes Cooking Time: 30-45 minutes Total Time: 35-50 minutes Servings: 2-3

Ingredients:
1 pound pork skin (removed from pork belly or shoulders)
Sea salt (optional)

Clean the pork skin: Thoroughly wash the pork skin and remove any excess fat or meat using a sharp knife.
Cut the skin: Cut the pork skin into small, bite-sized pieces.
Simmer the skin (optional): In a pot, cover the skin with water and bring to a simmer for 30 minutes. This step helps soften the skin and render some fat, but it's not necessary for achieving a crispy texture.
Dry the skin completely: Pat the pork skin pieces dry with paper towels. Ensure they are completely dry, as any moisture will prevent them from crisping properly.
Fry the skin: Heat enough lard or tallow in a deep fryer or heavy-bottomed pot to reach 350°F (175°C). Carefully add the pork skin pieces in small batches to avoid overcrowding the pot. Fry for 3-5 minutes, or until golden brown and puffed.
Drain and season: Remove the pork rinds with a slotted spoon and drain on paper towels to absorb excess oil. While still warm, sprinkle with sea salt, if desired.

Nutritional Information (per 1 oz serving):
Calories: 150-180
Fat: 13-16g
Protein: 10-12g
Carbs: 0g

Deviled Eggs

Prep Time: 5 minutes Cook Time: 12-15 minutes Total Time: 17-20 minutes Servings: 6

Ingredients:
6 large eggs
2 tablespoons softened butter or ghee
1/4 cup cooked, shredded meat (ground beef, chicken, or pork)
Salt and pepper to taste
Optional garnishes: chopped cooked bacon, chives

Hard boil the eggs: Place the eggs in a single layer in a saucepan and cover with cold water. Bring to a boil over high heat, then remove from heat and cover. Let sit for 12-15 minutes, then drain and rinse with cold water until cool enough to handle.
Peel the eggs: Peel the eggs carefully, separating the whites from the yolks.
Mash the yolks: In a bowl, mash the egg yolks with a fork until smooth.
Combine ingredients: Add the softened butter or ghee, shredded meat, salt, and pepper to the mashed yolks and mix well until combined.
Fill the egg whites: Spoon the yolk mixture into the empty egg whites. You can use a piping bag for a neater presentation.
Garnish (optional): Sprinkle with chopped cooked bacon and chives for an extra savory flavor.
Serve: Enjoy immediately or store in an airtight container in the refrigerator for up to 3 days.

Nutritional Information (per serving):
Calories: 180-200
Fat: 12-15g
Protein: 10-12g
Carbs: 0g

Garlic Parmesan Chicken Wings:

Prep Time: 10 minutes Cook Time: 40-50 minutes Total Time: 50-60 minutes Servings: 2-3

Ingredients:
1 pound whole chicken wings, separated at the joint (tips discarded, optional)
1 tablespoon melted tallow or ghee
1/2 teaspoon sea salt
1/4 teaspoon black pepper
1/4 cup grated Parmesan cheese

Preheat oven to 400°F (200°C). Line a baking sheet with parchment paper.
Pat the chicken wings dry with paper towels.
In a large bowl, toss the wings with melted tallow or ghee, salt, and pepper.
Arrange the wings in a single layer on the prepared baking sheet.
Bake for 30 minutes, then flip the wings and continue baking for another 10-20 minutes, or until the wings are golden brown and crispy and the internal temperature reaches 165°F (74°C).
In a small bowl, toss the hot wings with the grated Parmesan cheese.
Serve immediately.

Nutritional Information (per serving):
Calories: 450-500
Fat: 40-45g
Protein: 30-35g
Carbs: 0g

Salmon with Herb Butter

Prep Time: 5 minutes Cook Time: 10-12 minutes Total Time: 15 minutes Servings: 1

Ingredients:
1 (6-8 oz) skin-on salmon fillet
2 tbsp unsalted butter, softened
1 tbsp fresh chopped herbs (such as parsley, dill, or chives)
Salt and pepper to taste

Preheat oven to 400°F (200°C). Line a baking sheet with parchment paper.
In a small bowl, combine softened butter and chopped herbs. Season with salt and pepper to taste.
Place the salmon fillet skin-side down on the prepared baking sheet.
Spread the herb butter evenly over the flesh side of the salmon.
Bake for 10-12 minutes, or until the salmon is cooked through and flakes easily with a fork.

Nutritional Information:
(Based on a 3 oz serving of salmon and 2 tbsp butter)
Calories: 450
Fat: 35g
Protein: 40g
Carbs: 0g

SAUCES AND DIPS
Bang Bang Sauce

Prep Time: 5 minutes Cook Time: 5 minutes Total Time: 10 minutes Servings: 2

Ingredients:
2 tablespoons unsalted butter
2 tablespoons heavy cream
1 tablespoon sriracha (or to taste)
1/2 teaspoon red pepper flakes (or to taste)
Pinch of sea salt

In a small saucepan, melt the butter over medium heat.
Whisk in the heavy cream, sriracha, red pepper flakes, and sea salt.
Bring to a simmer and cook for 2-3 minutes, whisking occasionally, until slightly thickened.
Remove from heat and let cool slightly before using.

Nutritional Information (per serving):
Calories: 180
Fat: 16g
Protein: 1g
Carbs: 0g
Sugar: 0g

Buffalo Chicken Dip

Prep Time: 5 minutes Cooking Time: 20 minutes (depending on cooking method) Total Time: 25 minutes Servings: 4

Ingredients:
8 oz softened cream cheese
1 cup shredded cheddar cheese
1/2 cup cooked, shredded chicken breast
1/4 cup buffalo sauce (choose a sugar-free variety)
1 tablespoon melted butter or ghee
Salt and pepper to taste

In a medium bowl, combine cream cheese and cheddar cheese. Mix until well combined.
Add cooked, shredded chicken, buffalo sauce, and melted butter. Stir until evenly incorporated.
Season with salt and pepper to taste.
Transfer the mixture to a small baking dish or oven-safe ramekin.
Bake at 375°F (190°C) for 20-25 minutes, or until bubbly and lightly browned on top.
Serve immediately with your preferred dippers like pork rinds, celery sticks, or jicama slices.

Nutritional Information (per serving):
Calories: 450
Fat: 35g
Protein: 30g
Carbs: 0g
Fiber: 0g

Steak Fajita Marinade

Prep Time: 5 minutes Cooking Time: 10-15 minutes Total Time: 15-20 minutes Servings: 2

Ingredients:
1 lb ribeye steak, thinly sliced
Sea salt
Black pepper

In a bowl, toss the sliced steak with sea salt and black pepper to taste.
Marinate the steak for at least 5 minutes, or up to overnight, in the refrigerator.
Heat a cast iron skillet or grill pan over medium-high heat.
Sear the steak for 2-3 minutes per side, or until desired doneness is reached.
Serve immediately with your favorite fajita toppings, like chopped onions and peppers (not carnivore-compliant).

Nutritional Information (per serving):
Calories: 520
Fat: 45g
Protein: 50g
Carbs: 0g

Teriyaki Sauce

Prep Time: 5 minutes Cooking Time: 10 minutes Total Time: 15 minutes Servings: 2

Ingredients:
2 tablespoons beef broth
1 tablespoon water
1 tablespoon apple cider vinegar (optional, for extra tang)
1/2 teaspoon ground ginger
1/4 teaspoon garlic powder
1/4 teaspoon onion powder
Pinch of sea salt
Pinch of black pepper

In a small saucepan, combine beef broth, water, apple cider vinegar (if using), ginger, garlic powder, onion powder, salt, and pepper.
Bring the mixture to a simmer over medium heat.
Reduce heat to low and simmer gently for 10 minutes, allowing the flavors to meld.
Remove from heat and let cool slightly before using.

Nutritional Information: (per serving)
Calories: 10
Fat: 0g
Carbs: 0g (including fiber)
Protein: 2g

Garlic Parmesan Sauce

Prep Time: 5 minutes Cook Time: 5 minutes Total Time: 10 minutes Servings: 2

Ingredients:
2 tablespoons unsalted butter
2 cloves garlic, minced
1/2 teaspoon dried rosemary
1/4 teaspoon dried thyme
Salt and black pepper to taste

In a small saucepan over medium heat, melt the butter.
Add the garlic and cook until fragrant, about 30 seconds.
Stir in the rosemary and thyme, and cook for another 30 seconds.
Remove from heat and season with salt and pepper to taste.

Nutritional Information (per serving):
Calories: 190
Fat: 14g
Protein: 0g
Carbs: 0g

Honey Garlic Sauce

Prep Time: 5 minutes Cook Time: 5 minutes Total Time: 10 minutes Servings: 2

Ingredients:
2 tablespoons grass-fed butter
4 cloves garlic, minced
1/4 cup water or bone broth
1 tablespoon soy sauce (optional, omit for stricter carnivore compliance)
1/2 teaspoon stevia extract (or other carnivore-friendly sweetener to taste)
Pinch of black pepper

Heat butter in a skillet over medium heat until melted and starting to brown.
Add garlic and cook for 30 seconds, until fragrant.
Stir in water or bone broth, soy sauce (if using), stevia, and black pepper.
Bring to a simmer and cook for 2-3 minutes, allowing the sauce to thicken slightly.
Remove from heat and serve immediately over your favorite carnivore-compliant dish, like grilled steak, chicken, or fish.

Nutritional Information (per serving):
Calories: 120
Fat: 11g
Protein: 1g
Carbs: 3g (including 1 g from stevia)

TIPS AND TRICKS FOR PERFECT AIR FRIED CARNIVORE MEALS

Here are some tips and tricks for making the best air-fried meat dishes:

Before you start cooking:

- Dry-pat your meat: If the meat's top has too much water, it won't get crispy. Before you season or air fry your meat, use paper towels to wipe off any extra water from the surface.

- Add a lot of seasoning: Since meat-based meals don't usually have marinades or sauces, it's important to use a lot of salt, pepper, and any other spices you want. Try out different mixes of spices to find the ones you like best.

- Preheat your air fryer (optional): Before cooking, you don't have to, but it can help make the crust crispier, especially for meat that is heavier.

While cooking:

- Don't overcrowd the basket: This will prevent proper air movement and lead to uneven cooking and less crispy results. Cook your meat in batches if necessary.

- Flip for even cooking: Depending on the thickness of your meat, you may need to flip it halfway through cooking to ensure even browning and doneness.

- Shake the basket (optional): Gently shaking the basket halfway through cooking can help spread the heat and promote even burning.

Tips for specific cuts:

- Steaks: For bigger cuts like ribeye or New York Strip, preheating your air fryer is suggested. Sear the steaks at a high temperature (around 400°F) for a few minutes per side to make a crust, then drop the temperature to finish cooking to your chosen doneness.

- Ground meat: Form ground meat into burgers and cook at a low setting (around 375°F) until cooked through. You can also use the air oven to cook broken ground meat for recipes like tacos or chili.

- Chicken wings: For crispy wings, toss them in baking powder or cornstarch before air frying. This will help draw out wetness and promote crispiness. Cook at a high temperature (around 400°F) until golden brown and cooked through.

- Fatty cuts: Fatty cuts like pork belly benefit from being cooked skin-side down originally. The drained fat will help crisp up the skin.

Additional tips:

- Use an instant-read thermometer: This is the most effective way to ensure your meat is cooked to the proper temperature.

- Consult your air fryer manual: Cooking times can change based on the specific type and power of your air fryer. Refer to the instructions for suggested cooking times and temperatures for different types of meat.
Experiment and have fun! The beauty of air cooking is its flexibility. Don't be afraid to try with different cuts of meat, spices, and cooking times to find what works best for you.

Conclusion

As you embark on your carnivorous culinary journey with the "Carnivore Air Fryer Cookbook," may each sizzling, succulent bite bring you unparalleled satisfaction? This cookbook is not just a collection of recipes; it's a guide to transforming your kitchen into a carnivore haven, where the air fryer becomes your trusted ally in crafting mouthwatering, nutrient-dense meals.

In the world of carnivore cooking, simplicity meets indulgence, and every dish is a celebration of the rich flavors and textures that come from quality meats. From crispy bacon to perfectly seared steaks, this cookbook has taken you on a gastronomic adventure that transcends traditional cooking boundaries.

Remember, the true essence of the carnivore lifestyle is not just about what you eat, but the joy and fulfillment it brings to your table. As you savor the last page of this cookbook, let it be a reminder that the power to create extraordinary meals lies in your hands – and in the hum of your trusty air fryer.

May your kitchen forever echo with the sizzle of satisfaction and the aroma of carnivorous delights? Here's to elevating your carnivore experience and savoring every delicious moment. Happy cooking!

Printed in Great Britain
by Amazon